Beginning with

Bettas

2nd edition

Bob Hole

ISBN-10: **1986675599**
ISBN-13: **978-1986675598**

DEDICATION

To Rusty, the betta that inspired this.

And my nieces.

Contents

Introduction 1

What is a betta? 2

where are bettas from? 3

Why are they called fighting fish? 4

how long do bettas live? 5

how do bettas breathe? 7

what do bettas eat? 9

how much should I feed my betta? 11

How much light does my betta need? 13

what should I keep my betta in? 14

what do i need to keep a betta? 17

how do I set up my betta aquarium? 21

when can i add my fish? 24

what happens after I set up the aquarium? 26

how do I clean my betta's aquarium? 28

what do I do if the water gets cloudy? 29

what do I do if my betta gets sick? 30

after all that, now what? 32

about the author 33

A male red and blue betta.

Introduction

There is a lot of information out there about keeping bettas, also called Siamese Fighting Fish. A lot of that information is wrong. Even some pet stores that ought to know better are giving out bad advice. Hopefully this publication will help you begin right and keep your betta in good health.

I will assume a couple things in this book. I'll assume you want to keep a betta. I will assume you are going to keep a male betta - the ones with the fancy fins. Many people keep female bettas. They don't fight, and they come in all the same fancy colors as males do, but they don't have the long fancy fins, so most people keep males. Therefore, when referring to "your" betta, I'm going to call him a him. But all the information for males works for the females - with one exception. You can usually keep more than one female in a tank.

You can sometimes even keep a male and female together. I'll give you more information how, later in the book.

What is a betta?

There are about 73 species (different kinds) of betta, though most of them are not kept in aquariums. The one species we see regularly in pet stores is *Betta splendens*. This is the species with bright colors of blue, red, green and yellow, and sometimes other colors, and where the males generally have fancy flowing fins.

Some of the other species of betta are quite beautiful, but not usually brightly colored. They certainly don't have the range of color and long fins as the domestic betta.

Like dogs, cats, and goldfish, domestic bettas (all *Betta splendens*) have been bred for specific traits that crop up in the population. This breeding has produced the amazing diversity of the modern aquarium betta. Not as big a diversity as the goldfish, yet, but then goldfish keeping has almost a thousand years "head start" on the betta keepers.

where are bettas from?

Wild bettas live in Thailand and surrounding parts of Southeast Asia, centered around the Mekong river valley. Thailand used to be called Siam, so bettas are sometimes called Siamese Fighting Fish.

Bettas have been kept as pets for so long, and in so many places, that it is now uncertain where they were originally native to and where they have been introduced, either accidentally or on purpose. The fish are very good at eating mosquito larvae, so they have been introduced in several places around the world for pest control.

There have been "wild" populations (starting as escaped or dumped pets) in the United States in Connecticut and Florida, but they are they probably extinct in both places.

Any betta you find in a pet store will have a long legacy of being bred for beauty of color and fins. Like goldfish, they're really no longer wild fish, but only captive animals, and it would be a great disservice to them if you were to dump them in a local pond or stream.

Why are they called fighting fish?

In the wild, bettas live in small streams, ponds, and drainage ditches where there is not much room and not much food. Bettas are at least somewhat territorial and they will fight with each other to keep other bettas out of their territory.

Wild bettas, though, are not nearly as territorial as captive fishes. Our fish were originally bred not for their beauty, like they are in most places, but for their fighting ability. The "best" fish, the fish that were bred, were the ones that were more aggressive. This tendency has not been bred out of the fish in the time they've been kept primarily for their beauty.

Some original stock of fighting fish gave rise to mutants with longer fins and brighter colors. These fish are the ancestors of our pet bettas, which have been bred for the longest fins or for some other trait than fighting ability.

They still are bred for fighting in some parts of the world. In the U.S. and U.K., along with many other countries, fighting the fish for sport is illegal.

how long do bettas live?

Bettas live about two years. A really old betta is a three year old. I've heard of a four year old fish, but that's a real exception. Most fish you might buy at a pet store are between three months and one year of age.

Assuming you keep your fish well and healthy, you can expect to keep your fish for one to two years. If yours lives longer, you're really doing something right!

A red and blue male betta.

how do bettas breathe?

Like all fish, bettas have gills. They take water in through their mouth and push it through two slits on the sides of their heads. Those slits lead to the gills between the mouth and the slits.

The gills act sort of like our lungs. They are thin tissues with lots of small blood vessels in them. As the water passes over the tissues, oxygen diffuses from the water into the blood, and carbon dioxide and other wastes leave the blood and get swept out with the water through the gill slits.

If you watch a betta, you'll see their gills covers moving, and might catch a glimpse of the pink gills.

Bettas are special though! Unlike most other fishes, bettas have something called a labyrinth organ. The labyrinth organ lets them use air that they swallow from the surface of the water - that's why they come up to the top a lot. Once they swallow the air, rather than going into the stomach, it goes into the labyrinth organ, which pulls oxygen into the blood and pushes carbon dioxide out of the body, again similar to our lungs.

Having both gills and a labyrinth organ means that bettas can breathe in both air and water. But they need both too. If you somehow prevent a betta from coming to the surface, it will drown. And if you take a betta out of the water it will suffocate.

Having both gills and a labyrinth organ also means that bettas can live in water that has very little oxygen in it. This means they can live in stagnant water or in very small containers. It does not mean that such conditions are good for the fish.

A dwarf gourami. Gouramis also have a labyrinth organ and can breathe air like bettas, but they need more room and higher temperatures than bettas.

what do bettas eat?

Bettas are carnivores and eat mostly meat. They eat small invertebrates and very small fishes that live around them. They also eat small insects that fall into the water.

In many places they live in the wild this is the only source of food, so they have the habit of spending a lot of time floating near the surface of the water, though a healthy fish will swim all around his aquarium. In the wild they eat many mosquito larvae, which also spend their time at the surface of the water.

In the aquarium, bettas will eat flake food or "betta pellets" (though some pet stores will tell you they "must" eat these pellets, they do just fine on other carnivorous fish foods).

They will also eat frozen or live brine shrimp and bloodworms, and enjoy these as a treat. Again, some stores will try to sell you live bloodworms, saying bettas only eat these worms. That is not true. In fact a steady diet of worms will make the fish fat and they will die prematurely.

They'll even take these foods freeze-dried, but might have to learn to eat them. They're really not too picky about what they eat. But don't feed them too much plant-based foods like goldfish food, at least very often.

Small aquatic animals like this mosquito larvae are favorite foods of wild bettas.

how much should I feed my betta?

Bettas are not active fish and don't need a lot of food. They should not be fed large amounts, especially if you're keeping them in a small aquarium. Feed no more than your fish can eat in five minutes.

It's better to feed bettas in the morning, because then they have all day to find any food they miss at first. But you can feed him any time he'll have between fifteen and 30 minutes with lights on around him. Any shorter time means your fish may miss something and the food may rot overnight.

One neat thing about fish is that it's okay if you forget to feed your fish for a day or two, or need to go on a vacation for the weekend. Your betta can go a couple days without food. It's not something you should forget every week, but if you forget once in a while, it's just fine!

In the wild, they wouldn't eat every day, so irregularly forgetting to feed your pet won't do him any harm.

A betta can even go a whole week without food once in a while if you're going on a long vacation. You should never feed him "extra" food though, either before you leave or after you return, it'll just rot in the tank and make the water gray and smelly.

Because you should be taking care already to not overfeed your fish, if you keep him in a small bowl by himself you shouldn't make him go more than about a week without food. Teach any substitute fish feeder how to feed your fish.

A very nice all red male betta.

How much light does my betta need?

Bettas don't need much light, just enough to see the things in the tank and to find any food around them. You don't need a light on the top of their aquarium except to see your betta. If you have one turn it off when you're not watching the fish.

If the light is on too much, green algae (little plants) will grow on the sides of the tank and you'll have to clean it to see inside. Algae won't hurt the fish, but most people just think it doesn't look pretty.

Also, with small bowls especially, if you leave a warm light on too long, it will overheat the water and might kill the fish.

what should I keep my betta in?

Bettas are very easy fish to keep, and they can live in very little water so their aquarium can be just about any size or shape. However, keeping your fish in the little plastic bowl sometimes provided by the pet store is not a good idea.

There are disadvantages to keeping a betta in a very small amount of water. First, the water will get dirty fast. You may even need to change the water every day. This is a hassle for most people, and it soon loses its charm.

Second, the water conditions change faster in a small body of water. The temperature, water chemistry, and oxygen levels can change in minutes in a pint or quart container. This will stress the fish, making it more likely to come down with a disease or even shorten its lifespan.

I strongly recommend an aquarium or bowl of at least one gallon (3.8 L). This is the smallest amount of water that allows you to really sit back and enjoy your fish. The tank will need to be cleaned less often, and your fish will be able to move around. He will also be more relaxed and less stressed, meaning he will be healthier.

You can keep bettas in larger tanks of course, I like to keep them in tanks about two gallons (8 L) if I'm keeping them alone, but I've kept them with other fish in up to a fifty gallon (190 L) tank, but still only one male betta per tank.

I have read of someone keeping four male bettas in a 100 gallon (380 L) tank, but none of the fishes looked very pretty.

Despite their name of fighting fish, bettas can be kept with other fishes. They don't fight with fish other than other bettas, and get along with many other kinds. I don't recommend guppies or tetras, however, as companions for bettas. Bettas are slow fishes with long fins, and tetras and guppies are fast fish that tend to bite at those long fins. Some people will tell you they do fine together, often they do, but I prefer not to take the risk.

Nipped fins may not seem important but they are part of the fish's body, not like hair. Wounds to the fins are like wounds anywhere else on the fish and can lead to infection.

If you want to keep a female betta with your male, you can. You need at least a two gallon aquarium, though five gallons would be better. You also need to make sure you have two or three plants the female can hide behind if she needs to. Males can sometimes be aggressive even toward females. It helps if you can add the male and female betta to the tank at the same time. It doesn't always work, and sometimes the male will kill the female – or more rarely the female will kill the male. But it's possible to do.

It's not likely that your fishes will breed unless you keep them in really top-notch shape, but it's possible. In those cases the male builds a nest out of bubbles that float on the surface. Breeding and taking care of any young are beyond the scope of this introductory book, however.

A white betta. This looks like a short-finned male, but may be a female.

what do i need to keep a betta?

The things you absolutely need for keeping a betta are:

Aquarium to keep the water in. You can use just about anything that will hold water, but you should make sure it's got a large enough opening at the top so you can get things (like the fish, and maybe a small net) in and out, and steady enough to not rock around or tip over easily. Some people use wide-mouth bottles and jars (even a well cleaned two liter bottle with the top cut off would work - not ideal, but it could be done). Some people use fancy vases, and many other types of containers. Remember though, I strongly recommend at least one gallon of water. Since I also recommend a heater, I'll suggest a glass container unless you're using an aquarium from a pet store.

Water to keep the fish in. Most tap water is suitable to keep bettas in, using a water conditioner. Your local pet store should be able to tell you if this is not the case - but it would be not the case for ALL fishes. Selling "betta water" has sometimes become popular, but if you need special water for bettas, you need special water for all fishes. If they don't sell special water for guppies or goldfish, you don't need it for your betta.

Bettas can be kept in vases, and even with planted vases. But make sure the plants are fish-safe and pesticide free!

Water conditioner to remove Chloramines and/or Chlorine from tap water. These two chemicals are used to keep bacteria and other life forms from growing in our tap water. Good for us, but they also keep fish from living in our tap water. Exposure to either of them can kill a fish very quickly. Always use a water conditioner BEFORE you put the fish in the water. Usually it acts to instantly neutralize the Chloramines or Chlorine, but read and follow the directions. Also usually, it's okay if you add too much of the conditioner, you just don't want to add too little.

Food to feed the fish. See the section on feeding your betta to find out what kind of food.

Things you should consider having for keeping a betta are:

Water Heater for keeping the temperature around 78°F (25.5 C), the temperature bettas are comfortable at. If you keep them too cool, they will eventually get sick and die prematurely. Some stores may say you can keep them at room temperature, but with more and more people keeping their rooms at 68°F (20 C), you really should invest in a heater. That is just too cold for most aquarium fishes (goldfish excepted).

A **thermometer** may be needed for your aquarium if you have a heater. Some heaters come with a built in thermometer or are preset, so you may not need a separate thermometer. If you have a larger aquarium (five gallons [19 L] or more) I always suggest putting the thermometer as far away from the heater as possible. This lets you know that the heat is getting everywhere in the tank.

Water filter of some kind. This keeps the water cleaner, longer. It does not replace general maintenance of the aquarium, but it helps keep it to a minimum. There are in-tank filters, and hang-on-the-side filters, and built-into-the-hood filters. Most of filters for aquariums of a gallon or two work in the same way - water is pumped over or through some material and returned to the tank. The filter captures much of the waste of the fish, either the solid waste or the liquid waste. The carbon in the filter captures the liquid waste. It doesn't capture it all, which is why you'll do water changes, but it helps out a lot. The filter material the water is pumped through is replaced about once a month. Make sure your pet store carriers replacement filter pads. I recently had to reject buying four filters for a new aquarium set-up because the store that wanted to sell them to me couldn't sell me replacement filter pads!

"Under-gravel" filters are perforated plastic plates that are put on the bottom of a bowl or tank, under a layer of gravel. For a bowl-sized under-gravel filter, an air pump is used to circulate the water down through the gravel and pull waste down. You don't need to change the gravel, but you do need to stir it up whenever you do a water change.

Dedicated water scoop, or ladle. This is for taking water out and putting water in to the aquarium. You don't want to use the same utensil for your soup that you use for your fish. The problem is not that you might get something from the fish, but that you should never use soap on anything you use for the aquarium. The type of scoop depends a lot on the size of the aquarium, and the size of the opening. You might need a ladle, or you might just need a small plastic container as a scoop. You could also get some sort of "aquarium vacuum", however, most of these move five gallons or more water a minute - much too much for a small betta aquarium.

A different kind of food. Eating macaroni and cheese every day might sound fun, but it's kind of boring. Be kind to your betta and give him a varied diet. See the section on feeding bettas to see what kinds of foods you might consider. Even two different kinds of flakes can make eating more exciting for the fish.

An **aquarium light**, like I mentioned above, is really something that is for you. Unless you keep live plants, it's so you can see the fish. The betta is fine with light from the room around it. Though if you keep your aquarium in a dark corner, or feed him at odd hours, you may need a light placed near the aquarium so he can see to eat, too. Usually if you're happy with the light level in the room, so is your betta.

Decorations, like gravel, plants (plastic, silk, or live), rocks, castles, whatever you fancy. The fish don't need these, though a plant or two might make them feel more comfortable if the aquarium is in a busy area. These really can fit the decor of your room, be naturalistic, or be wild and imaginative. Remember your betta is a descendent of a long line of aquarium bred fish - the natural habitat for a betta is now an aquarium, so feel free to put in that mermaid castle or sunken pirate ship.

how do I set up my betta aquarium?

The first thing you should do is decide where to place the aquarium. It should be a location secure and strong enough to prevent it falling off. Water weighs about 8 lbs per gallon (1 kg per 1 L), and whatever you place your tank on must be able to support that weight, and a location not too near a window (too much light, plus extra heat or cold depending on the season).

It should also not be too near air conditioning or heating ducts, for similar reasons that you don't want it right by a window.

The aquarium should also be near an electrical outlet so you can plug in the heater, filter, light, and anything else that may require electricity. I recommend using a surge protector with any aquarium. If you have electrical cords leading from the aquarium, try to have them loop up at some point before they get to the plug. This allows any water drip off them, and not reach the electrical system.

Having picked the location, you're ready to set things up.

You should first rinse the aquarium out. There are sometimes residues left over from making aquariums, or from sitting in the shop that could be harmful to fishes. This rinsing should be thorough, but you shouldn't need to scrub it strongly.

Remember to never use any soap on the aquarium or anything that goes into it. Soap residue can coat the gills of fish and cause them to suffocate. If you need to use something to scrub the aquarium or anything else, you can use plain non-iodized salt. You can get this from the grocery store. Make sure and rinse it off well.

Once your aquarium is rinsed, fill it about two thirds (2/3) of the way with water. The water should be a bit warm to the touch, If you have an aquarium thermometer, try to aim to get the water to about 78ºF (25.5 C).

Rinse and put any gravel you might use into the aquarium. Rinsing gravel can take a while, you need to try and get as much dust out of it as you can, and some aquarium gravels are very dusty. You can use a kitchen sieve or colander to do this. Make sure you rinse the dish extremely well before putting in the gravel. This is about the only case where using something that's come in contact with soap is okay.

Set up the filter, heater, and anything else you need to put in the aquarium. How you set these up depends on what kinds you get, so refer to the packages.

If you're setting up the aquarium with decorations, those should also be rinsed well, and can now be put in the aquarium.

Once you've got all that set up, you can fill the tank the rest of the way, to about a half inch below the top of the container. Add your water conditioner to remove the Chlorine or Chloramines in the tap water, plug in and start the heater and the filter, and you're all set.

Now the hard part. Don't add your fish.

You can decorate your betta aquarium any way you want. As long as it's warm enough, a betta could be quite happy in this size bowl.

when can i add my fish?

Once your aquarium is set up you should wait at least 24 hours before adding your fish. This means you shouldn't even bring the fish home before that time. Longer is fine, so if you set up your aquarium on one weekend and go find a fish the next weekend that works well for all involved.

This delay allows time to make sure everything is working properly, that the aquarium doesn't have a leak, and for the water to "settle". Water fresh out of the tap has a lot of extra air mixed into it. As the water settles, the extra air forms little bubbles that can stick to the any surface in the aquarium including fishes. Gradually the bubbles rise to the surface and pop.

During the first 24 hours, the heater is settling in, and bringing your aquarium up to 78ºF (25.5 C), or letting it cool to that if the water you added was too warm. Also the filter is working and changing the water chemistry in the tank just a little bit.

Added all together these little changes can create stress on a new fish in the aquarium. Changing from one aquarium (at the store) to your home aquarium is going to be stress enough on the fish. Too much stress can make a fish ill or even kill it, so by waiting we reduce the risk to the fish.

Once you've waited about 24 hours, you can go ahead and put the fish in the aquarium. Try to put as little water from the store into your aquarium as you can. A small fish net can help you do this, otherwise, just try to add very little. The water that you bring your fish home in is probably relatively dirty, and is definitely different than the water in your new tank. Adding it to the aquarium can cause some problems, so it's better to limit those problems by adding as little as possible.

what happens after I set up the aquarium?

After your fish is in the aquarium there will be several changes to the tank, most of them unseen by you. The most important of these is that there are bacteria which will grow in the tank to help keep it clean. These bacteria are responsible for the nitrogen cycle, which is very important to the health of the fish.

During the first week or so, the fish waste in the aquarium will start to build up. This is normal, and shouldn't cause any problem if you've just got one fish and at least a gallon of water. The fish waste is in the form of ammonia and is poisonous to fish, which is why they get rid of it from their bodies, we do too. There are bacteria that eat ammonia. These bacteria will colonize your aquarium and break down the fish waste. They are just about everywhere, so don't worry about adding any. They'll find your tank.

These ammonia eating bacteria turn the ammonia into a substance called nitrites. These are just as poisonous as the ammonia, but there are other kinds of bacteria that eat those nitrites. As the nitrites build up in the aquarium, these bacteria colonize it, and start eating the nitrites. They turn the nitrites into nitrates.

Some sources will tell you that nitrates are not poisonous to fishes, but they are. They are just VERY much less poisonous to the fish. You'd have to add a lot of nitrates for the fish to be stressed enough to do it a lot of harm. And you won't ever come close to that harm if you regularly clean the aquarium and do a change of water.

This whole process of the nitrogen cycle getting started in your tank takes about three weeks. During that time it's very important you don't overfeed your betta. Overfeeding will let other bacteria move in and disrupt the start of the nitrogen cycle.

A double-tail male betta. Note that it does have two separate tails.

how do I clean my betta's aquarium?

Assuming you have an aquarium of at least one gallon, about once a month you should change some of the water in the aquarium. I recommend you change about 25% of the water. This is what the ladle or other scoop-container is for.

I also recommend that you use a chopstick or other implement to stir up the gravel on the bottom of the aquarium a bit before you scoop out about a quarter of the water. Stirring up the gravel allows any solid waste trapped there to float up into the water, so you might scoop it up, or the filter will be able to deal with it. This is particularly important if you're using an under-gravel filter.

You can then add new water from the tap to top up your aquarium. Try to make sure the water is about the same temperature as the aquarium water is. This will stress the fish less. Also make sure to add your water conditioner to the water before adding it to the aquarium.

That's really all you should need to do to clean the aquarium.

what do I do if the water gets cloudy?

If the water gets cloudy gray right after you set up your aquarium, that usually means the gravel wasn't quite cleaned well enough. Usually changing half the water and waiting a day or two clears things up.

If the water gets cloudy gray after you've had the tank up and running for a while, that means you're feeding too much and your betta can't find all the food fast enough to eat it. If that happens, don't feed your betta for three days (he'll be fine!). If the water isn't clear by then, feed your betta once, then don't feed him again for three days. If that doesn't clear up the water, you will need to do a water change, probably of about 50%. Otherwise follow the instructions for cleaning the aquarium, and feed the fish a little less.

what do I do if my betta gets sick?

Bettas are generally healthy fish. Look for three things to see if your betta is sick. These things are rare but are the most common problems seen.

1. Are the ends of his fins turning white and a little fuzzy? This is called "fin rot". It means he has a fungus on his fins, and you'll need to get a medicine from the pet store. The people at the store can recommend the best one. Some fish have white at the edges of their fins and that's their regular color. Just watch if the white looks like it's spreading or is fuzzy.

2. Are there little white dots all over your betta, like someone sprinkled him with salt? This is called "ick". The white spots are little animals that sometimes live on fish skin. You'll need to get some medicine from the pet store. Again, the people at the store can recommend the best one. One that I've used and recommend is aquarium salt. Add about a teaspoon per gallon and that should be enough. After a few days if the spots grow in number, you'll need something stronger.

3. Is the body of the betta getting fat so that the scales are sticking out? This is a bacterial disease called dropsy. There are medications for it, but I've successfully used a teaspoon of salt per gallon of water, and changing 50% of the water before adding it. bettas get dropsy much more frequently than other fishes do, possibly because they are usually in such small containers.

All of these illnesses can be fatal and treatment should be undertaken with that in mind.

Other things can kill your fish too. bettas can get something like most of the diseases that we can get, including heart attacks. If your fish dies, you may never know what kills him.

If your betta dies, rinse the aquarium and everything in it with very warm water and let it dry out for at least a day or two before setting up for a new fish.

Rusty, a red betta to whom this book is dedicated, in his aquarium.
Photo by the author.

after all that, now what?

Sit back, relax, and enjoy your new pet.

about the author

Bob Hole has been keeping fishes since 1967. He has a degree in Biology from Cal Poly, San Luis Obispo, California, and has done graduate work in Mississippi and New Mexico. Bob has worked for the California Department of Fish and Game and the U.S. Fish and Wildlife Service, as well at several museums around the country including the National Museum of Natural History (Smithsonian). He has presented academic and fun courses and talks, on a broad range of biology and natural history topics to audiences of all ages

Images courtesy pixabay.com

Made in United States
North Haven, CT
29 March 2023

34695200R00024